C000110237

How to
Groom's Speech

STEVE JOHNS

ISBN: 9798682599424

For all the grooms who don't know where to start.

I was that guy.

This one's for you.

CONTENTS

ACKNOWLEDGMENTS

Thanks to my amazing wife, Rach, for your unconditional support.

Chapter One

Introduction – My speech

It can feel daunting when you start writing your groom's speech, staring at a blank page with accumulating dread. You will have all of your friends and closest family in attendance and, naturally, you'll want to do yourself proud. This book will guide you in writing your own personalised groom's speech from start to finish, step-by-step.

I'd been a guest at many weddings where the groom stood up and ad-libbed. You could see the panic in their unprepared eyes as they were passed the microphone. They bumbled through their speech and were trying to remember who to thank off the top of their head. Don't be that guy.

I wanted to make my speech immaculate, so I put lots of effort into planning a template. I drafted and re-drafted my template three times. This preparation made the reading and the delivery of my groom's speech very easy. It's a fantastic feeling to sit down after your speech and know that you did everything you possibly could to make it the best it could have been.

I wanted to thank all the right people in my life and ensure I didn't forget anyone. By effectively planning your speech, you will not be caught short. As groom's speeches go, mine was longer than most would be. Personally, standing up and talking for longer was a small price to pay when it came to delivering the most important speech of my life. If you want to deliver a shorter speech, you can easily take the best bits from my template and shorten it.

You've bought this book to help you, therefore you've have taken a step that 99% of grooms haven't. I know that you are now ready and committed to make yours a success and are prepared to put in the effort.

At our wedding there were five soon-to-be-wed grooms in attendance. Within a month of giving my groom's speech, I'd had a few requests from some asking for support with their own speeches. This was reassuring, because it meant my speech couldn't have been that bad after all! After sending my speech via email and offering some advice, I realized that I could help many more people by breaking down my speech into manageable chunks, which has ended up as the book you're reading.

This book will help you write a groom's speech to be proud of. Together, we will create a speech that is personal to you and your wedding that will give you confidence in the lead up to your big day.

Have a pen and paper ready (or your laptop open) and get ready to write your speech. I will help you by explaining how of my own speech went on the day, with some anecdotes, advice and tips along the way. Use a highlighter to select bits that you want to include, and please make notes in the margins or on a pad as you go.

When I sat down to first write my speech, I was just like you, a guy trying to prevent messing it up. Now I speak to you from the other side, and I can reassure you that all will be ok if you're prepared.

Let's start your speech.

Chapter Two

What should the groom's speech include?

There are two essential things a groom's speech must do:

> 1) Thank the appropriate people
> 2) Tell his wife how much he loves her

If you simply do these two things, you will have delivered a successful speech.

Traditionally, the main three speeches at a wedding are given by:

1. The father of the bride
2. The groom
3. The best man

There are some exceptions to this rule due to family personnel and the scale of your wedding, but most weddings with a sit-down meal (wedding breakfast) will include the above in their order of the day.

The Father of the bride's speech

The father of the bride's speech is always up first. His speech will definitely have some anecdotes about his daughter from throughout her life, and say how beautiful she looks on the day. This is usually followed by a joke or two about how the groom met the bride's family, and how the groom has taken his pride and joy from him. Overall, his speech is brief, endearing, and will allow you to get a feel for the audience for your speech to come.

His speech will always end with a toast to the 'happy couple' or 'bride and groom'. It's worth speaking to the father of the bride beforehand if possible, as some like to keep their speech a secret until the day. It is worth asking them so you can cross-check material with your own speech to make sure you are not covering too much of the same ground. If the three main speeches flow from one to the other without too much repetition it makes the experience for the guests more interesting and engaging. Even if they politely decline your offer to discuss speeches, it's a considerate move to make.

During the father of the bride's speech, look around the room at the seating plan. Make a mental note of who is seated in which area of the room. If you need to address or reference different individuals during your speech make a mental note of where they are because knowing this will save you some stalling. Treat the father of the bride's speech like a crash test dummy – they are the trial run to test your audience!

You can get a feel for which of his jokes go down well and also how his vocals come over on the microphone. Make sure that in your speech you give thanks for his kind words; this will transition well into your speech. It is a good ideato have a joined-up approach to all the speeches, rather than give each speech as a separate episode.

The groom's speech

The groom's speech itself should be a tribute to a groom's love for his wife, and is an opportunity to say thank you to everyone that needs thanking. The groom should toast both the bridesmaids and the bride. Traditionally, the groom may wish to thank the host, the in laws, his parents and the groom's party (I did all the above in my speech).

Some brides may wish to take the opportunity (during your groom's speech) to toast her bridal party herself. My wife was happy for me to do the honours!

The best man's speech

This is often the most anticipated speech. Everyone wants to see the groom's mask slip, and all his polished and refined eloquence stripped back to who he really is. I'm sure that you're already a fine gent, but the best man's speech tends to show you in a different light, harping back to your school days or in your formative years as a young man. As a groom you need to revel in it - it's good fun! Remember, your best man will never want to genuinely ruin your day. And who knows, your best man might even say something nice about you!

Chapter Three

How to make an outline plan of your groom's speech

I found the best way to get creative is have a basic structure as the foundation of your speech. This structure can be shortened or lengthened as you wish, but will consist of the following headings:

- Welcome and General Opening
- Thanks to New In-laws (Mother and Father of the bride)
- Thanks to Own Mother and Father
- Thanks to Maid of Honour and Bridesmaids
- Thanks to Grooms Party
- Thanks to Pageboys, Flower Girls and Venue
- Speech about your Wife
- Introduction of Best Man

I start to detail this exact structure for my groom's speech in the next chapter. Each section of my speech will be explained in the chapters that follow. At a minimum this bullet point list is all you need for your speech. You could even put it on a sticky note!

I've never felt like a natural public speaker, and had never in front of friends and family. By following this process I was able to convince everyone I was calm, relaxed and knew what I was doing. I planned my speech as thoroughly as possible, and have put all my efforts into this book so you can reap the benefits. In that sense, I have gladly been your crash test dummy.

I felt more comfortable in having my speech written down word for word, which I read from printed paper on the day. By the end of this book, once you have written your speech you may feel like you know it well enough to write shorthand notes, or even write it on bullet points on a scrap of paper. If this is you, go for it. My process of planning will help you understand what you are trying to say and how you can actually say it, so it won't hurt to plan yours out in full.

As you are writing your speech, it helps to visualize delivering it. You need to remember that everyone in the room will be on your side, and that you will never have a more supportive audience. Guests will whoop, clap and encourage you, so be prepared for it!

My speech was delivered after the wedding breakfast (meal). After a few drinks, the guests were in great spirits and were very relaxed. When planning your wedding I highly recommend speaking after everyone has eaten. You know the crowd will be well satiated and will have a drink in hand, and will therefore be at ease. The danger of delivering your speech before everyone has eaten is that the crowd will be hungry therefore more restless.

I chose to read from printed sheets as I had a lot of people to thank and did not want to feel stuck for words. This made my speech slightly longer, but was a price I was willing to pay for getting my speech right and not missing any detail. It's your wedding day after all, so do what you feel comfortable with.

If you put yourself in the position of a guest at your wedding, they will likely be sitting at their table, sipping their drink, looking around the room and maybe whispering to others. Although you might feel like everyone's attention is on you, most guests are passive listeners and let their attention wander.

I was grateful for a microphone provided by the venue, so it's worth checking if you have access to one. A microphone allows you to speak at a natural volume, not shout. With this in mind I felt my delivery could be calm, relaxed, and yet still be heard by everyone clearly using my usual speaking voice. The temptation will be to speak loudly when using a microphone to make sure you are heard – remember there will be people by the speakers who won't thank you for it. You need to trust that your speech will be enjoyed more when you speak in a conversational tone. You will be more much more enjoyable to listen to.

The groom will mostly speak on behalf of his wife and himself during his speech. However, it's important to note that when a groom speaks to or about his bride he should speak for himself alone. The way the groom turns, their tone of voice, and their hand and face gestures all come into play, but that will come naturally with proper planning of your groom's speech. That's why you are reading this!

Get your pen and paper ready, you're about to start writing your speech.

Chapter Four

Welcome and general opening of your speech

I opened my speech with:

- *"Good afternoon everyone! We take great pleasure in welcoming you here for our special day... where the countdown is over... and we are now Mr & Mrs >**surname**<! (pause for applause!)"*

By saying 'Mr and Mrs >**surname**<' you will evoke a big cheer and definitely get a reaction. I continued:

- *"On behalf of my wife and I (!!!) We want to thank you all for being here with us on this special day, for all your good wishes, and for your wonderful gifts. People have travelled from various parts of the UK to be with us today... we have large groups of people from Cornwall and Devon, Essex and London, and the Midlands, among others".*

Mentioning 'my wife and I' will always get a merry cheer from those seasoned guests who have been eager for this phrase to be said! Recognizing the distances some have travelled, and if you pause at the end of saying each town/city and look up at the audience, you will invariably get cheers and noise from those who have travelled from those areas! This tactic builds rapport and gets the guests involved in a positive way.

Another popular way for grooms to open their speech is to thank the father of the bride for his kind words. It was slightly different for my wedding speech, as our 'father of the bride' speech was before the meal and there was some time between theirs and mine.

You would be wise to thank the father of the bride at this point, especially if they have just spoken and he has just handed you the microphone. I continued:

- *"For a while we've looked forward to bringing all the people that are special to us together, and now you're here, all scrubbed up and smelling nice. It's surreal for me to speak to you all at the same time. The fact that you are all here means everything to us.*

- *Just a bit of housekeeping – please make sure your glasses are charged for any toasts. Please stay in your seats for toasts from me – just raising a glass is fine! I have a few gifts to hand out later so when I do, a big clap would be great!"*

It's a good idea to instruct the guests as to what to do; it saves any awkwardness and the more nervous guests regarding correct etiquette will have been briefed. Also, while we are talking about toasts, it's obvious but please remember to say the toasts loudly and exactly as you want them to be heard. For example, *"A toast please, to, THE BRIDESMAIDS!"*

This will give your guests the cue to do the same. I have been to some weddings where there hasn't been an obvious cue to toast, and the speaker has just raised a glass and drank, leaving the guests unsure and mumbling their own version of a 'toast'. It looks and sounds, for want of a better word, unprofessional. Also with regard to toasts, telling the guests whether to stand up or sit down is important. Remember, as much as you might not want to, you need to direct the guests to do as you ask. You don't have to be formal about this, you could say, "*to save the musical chairs, I'd like you to…*".

When I wrote my speech down to use for the day, I used bullet points to distinctly separate statements. You could of course always shorten these. As I have mentioned, I read out all my points in full, which got my words across exactly as I had intended.

Chapter Five

Thanks to new in-laws

This part of your speech should give thanks to your new in-laws for welcoming you into the family. Now is your opportunity to show your appreciation to the bride's side of the family. With most families this is the case, but feel free to amend/shorten your speech if it is not!

For my speech, it was actually the mother of the bride who spoke before me and did the speech of 'father of the bride', due to my wife's father having passed away when she was younger. I made reference to this in my speech and made appropriate toasts later. You will work out how to structure this for yourself based on my layout below.

- *"I would like to thank >**mother of bride**< and >**mother of the bride's partner**< for making me feel a part of the family since day one, and I must thank >mother of the bride< for her kind words before the meal! You have always been an inspiration to me, to in your words 'never lose your sparkle'. It's clear to us all that >**bride**< and >**bride's sister**< have been fantastically brought up. You have been a rock to them both and you are clearly a very special lady. I am proud that I now officially have a second mum!"*

You may choose to then go on with an interesting anecdote about your induction into the family, or how you met. Mine was as follows:

- *"We holidayed as 'family >**family surname (e.g. Smith)**<' in Florida in the summer of 2012 .... It was incredible! One incident made me think I was truly part of the family.... (Mention key incident at the theme park and breaking the wine bottles in the evening – hope they have forgiven me!).*

- *>**mother of bride**< - You, >**mother of the bride's partner**< and >**bride's sister**< have all made me feel so welcome since the beginning and I am so lucky to have married your daughter today, who is the most beautiful person to me in every sense. I'd also like to say how wonderful both you and my own mum look today, and I'm sure everyone else agrees! (*cue cheers/whoops).*

- *I would now like us now to raise a toast to >**bride's**< father, >**bride's father (who is no longer with us)**<. Although I never had the pleasure of meeting him, I am told we are alike in many ways and I hope he would have approved of >**bride's**< choice of husband. I know he would be very, very proud of you. A toast please... to >**bride's father (who is no longer with us)**<. Thank you all.*

- *To Mum, Dad, >**mother of bride**< and >**mother of the bride's partner**<, Thank you* *for everything you've done towards making today a success. We really appreciate you being there for us and we wanted to give you a little something to thank you. *Hand presents*. A round of applause please for our family.*

Chapter Six

Thanks to own mother and father

This chapter will give you an opportunity to thank your own parents for everything they have done for you, not only for the wedding but also in your life so far. Of course, you can be the judge of what detail to go in here. It is always a nice touch to reveal a little about your upbringing, your relationship with your parents, and some anecdotes about your brothers and sisters. As you will see, I've put some personal detail in my speech that most will know to be true already (that I like rugby and I am also from Cornwall, England). The majority of guests will know you well and be able to identify with the things you say. Try to keep it general, with a few universally appreciated stories that every guest will be able to relate to. Here is what I wrote:

- *"Personally now, I'd like to say a thank you to my wonderful parents or, as I like to say in my strongest Cornish accent, **motheeeeer** and **faaather**! I owe so much to you both, all the evenings and the long trips to hundreds of rugby pitches across the country in my youth, and generally for kicking me out of bed in time for school.*

- *Dad- you have been an inspiration to me with your work ethic and drive to develop the business and you have put in some crazy hours, I still don't know how you got by with as little sleep! When I was a toddler Dad used to make me hot chocolate at 5.30am each morning before going to work. I am thankful for you and mum giving me the opportunity to pursue my passions of rugby and sport, which has led to a career in these fields.*

- *Mum, as I've said, you look amazing today. My main aim with this bit is to make you cry! You have always been the caring, rational, supportive and loving person watching over me and helping me with anything, from washing rugby kit, to your help with certain school projects. You too are an inspiration in so many ways. Thank you for everything.*

You can make this section as personal as you like. Some wish to simply say 'thank you' in a sentence, others will see it as an opportunity to publically say how much they appreciate their parents' contribution.

Chapter Seven

Thanks to maid of honour and bridesmaids

I started this section with:

- *"Now with ladies first, I would like to continue in traditional fashion by thanking our maid of honour, >**bride's**< sister, >**bride's sister's name**< and all of our bridesmaids. (**Addressing audience**) I know you'll all agree that they all look beautiful!" (cue some whooping and clapping by lifting the tone of your voice at the end of the sentence).*

By saying you would like to be traditional in your speech structure implies respect, and is also respectful of the formality of the speech. The best speeches I have ever seen in any situation acknowledge the formalities of the situation, yet play them down informally. If you want it to be more informal, you could simply say, "I would like to say thanks to…".

I continued:

- *"**>Bride's sister<** (**also Maid of honour**), you have always been with >**bride**< in both the good times **and** the tough times as her sister, and always been there for **us** both with advice, support and a lot of laughs. Thanks for everything you have done for us (including for our wedding), you have put in a great deal of work that we both appreciate. Also, to the bridesmaids >**Bridesmaid 1**< (my sister), >**Bridesmaid 2**< and >**Bridesmaid 3**<, thanks* *for all of your support for >**bride**<, she loves each of you dearly, and we value each of you immensely.*

- *>**Bridesmaid 1**<, 'sis', even though I still think you are 12 (and I still treat you like you're 12!!!), you have grown up into a beautiful young lady. Now you, >**bride**< and >**bride's sister**< are officially sisters! Ahh!*

- *We hope you enjoyed opening your gifts this morning with >**bride**<. A toast please… to… the bridesmaids!"*

Feel free to insert any anecdotes or funny stories. If you're in any doubt (with regard to making a remark about the bridal party), leave it out. It is not advisable to say anything 'tongue in cheek' or even slightly negative even as a joke. If you mention anything mildly controversial (even for comic effect) that is not flattering, always conclude on a heartfelt and genuine note to ensure you come across as being sincere and genuine in your affections. Doing this will be powerful and will mitigate any funny stories you may tell about them! They will have all put in a huge amount of effort in to the wedding preparations and to how they look on the day, so it will always go down well to thank and appreciate them for this. Remember, if in doubt, leave it out!

Chapter Eight

Thanks to groom's party

Having thanked the bridesmaids, you now have the license to be more light-hearted when talking about your own ushers and best man! You may feel yourself loosening up and getting more comfortable in your speech by now. Essential formalities done, this is where you can take it to a new level in terms of your warmth and humor. As with the bridesmaids, any light hearted comment or funny story should be immediately followed by a genuine and heartfelt word of appreciation for your closest friends. If you do this, the recipient of the initial joke will know that you genuinely care, and haven't just taken advantage of them for comic effect. It is a chance to say genuinely nice things about them (which you may not do to their face all that often!).

Here's how I did it:

- *"Onto my groom's party today. They are all here for their companionship; clearly not for their brains or beauty!"*

A lot of the audience jeered, which se the tone nicely for this section. A friendly comment like this isn't always necessary but I thought it was appropriate for my groomsmen. I go on to say:

- *">**Best man**<, thanks for everything you have done in preparation for today, including an incredible stag do in >**place name**<. >**Best man**<, we go back to our primary school days* *playing football against each other for >school name<! We were part of the infamous Backstreet Boys tribute dance group in a school concert (addressing audience) - I am still as shocked as you lot are! We have been solid mates for a long time. We may not have seen each other as much as we'd have liked to because of where we've lived recently.... but whenever we meet up it is as if no time has passed. (Addressing audience) Believe it or not, >Best man< has worked as a manager for L'Oréal shampoo. I'd like to say thanks for being my best man by giving you a little something too. Because you're worth it. Cheers mate". *Hand present*.*

You will have a story of how you met your best man or even one where he has been a fool, so you could always use this before you praise him in any way, or thank him for his efforts. I continued:

- *"Thanks also to my ushers- my brother >Usher 1<, then there's >Usher 2< and >Usher 3<. You guys have been fantastic not only today but throughout my life as mates".*

You could choose to keep it brief and leave it here, as this so far would suffice as a bare minimum. I chose to thank my groom's party in more detail as I felt the audience would enjoy it and I would like to take the opportunity to publicly recognize them.

- *>Usher 1, also my brother<, it means so much that you could be my usher today. I want to thank you for always being there to support me and scrap with me (and beat me up many times).You* *watched over me like a hawk as I cut the lawn (as a quality assurance measure of course), and generally looked after all things in the business when dad went 'gallivanting' on his rugby away days (*turn to dad* you still do that don't you?). A 3 hour trip to where we live is apparently 'do-able in a day!'. >Usher 1<, we had some great times growing up spending days out with cousins (all of which are here today!) with Granny, Grampy, Granddad and our <u>amazing</u> Grandma and Auntie Sylvia. Hi Grandma and Auntie Sylvia! >Usher 1<, you have been caring and kind - >bride< loves the fact she now has a brother! *Hand present*.*

- *>Usher 2<, when you arrived at >secondary school name< in Year 9... with long blonde golden locks (*audience should now laugh as he is now bald*).... you were the quickest kid on a rugby pitch I had ever seen, and had a thick northern accent. Where's that gone!? We had some great times throughout school, at Uni and ever since then. You can all ask >Usher 2< later to see pictures of his infamous 'dreadlock' phase. It will be well worth it I promise you! Please accept my gift as a thank you. *Hand present*.*

- *>Usher 3<, you've been there since I started working at >insert workplace< – you and >insert girlfriend's name< have been great friends to >bride< and I. You have always been there at the drop of a hat, and along with >other colleague< and >other colleague< you have made sure I have stayed sane at work – and made sure that I have a laugh too! Not only have <u>**we**</u> enjoyed your* *company, but we have a golden Labrador who also loves you very much! (It's a good job too, because you're the one that convinced us to get him!). Please may I give you a little something for being my usher today.* ****Hand Present****

- *A toast please, to ... the groom's party".*

Chapter Nine

Thanks to pageboys, flower girls and venue

If you have them at your wedding, now is the time to thank the pageboys and flower girls. I said:

- *"May I also say a big thanks to our beautiful flower girls for helping us today! >**flower girl 1**<, >**flower girl 2**< and >**flower girl 3**<.... you all look amazing. A round of applause please for the flower girls! We are so happy that we have so many children at our wedding; you really make it special. We have got to know each of you and seen you grow up!".*

We chose to include a brief thanks for our venue and caterers as we felt they did a fantastic job. It is polite to, but not essential. I give a brief anecdote below:

- *"We wanted to thank the >**venue name**< for hosting our wedding today. We've been in awe of the place since we first saw it! Also thanks to >**catering company name**<, our amazing caterers today. That roast beef was amazing! By the way, we went to a 'taster' day to 'sample' our food - I had one of those joints of beef to myself and I couldn't breathe after!!! In appreciation for both our venue and caterers please could we give a round of applause".*

Chapter Ten

Speech about your wife

Now the main formalities are said and done, the last and most important part of your speech is to say a heartfelt piece about your beautiful wife. This is the most important part of the speech and is what people will remember the speech for. It is a big opportunity to tell the world how much she means to you, hence this should be the part you put the most thought into. Please note, my section about my wife was probably on the long side, but I felt it was completely worth it as it was my time to say what I felt about her to all the friends and family that were listening. For your speech, you could shorten this section considerably. It should be a minimum of about three or four sentences. I started:

- *"Most importantly today, I wanted to thank >**Bride's new, full married name**< for agreeing to marry me! As >**mother of the bride**< has already said, she is beautiful, she's kind, she's caring and loving... and I still can't believe how lucky I am to now be able to call her my wife!*

Most audiences will at least give an 'Ahh' or at most give a round of applause. If this happens, let it! Enjoy the moment and don't rush through it. I continued:

- ***addressing bride*** *>**bride**<, "I want to take this moment to share some of our story so far with everyone. (addressing audience) Don't panic!*

- *We met through mutual friends at University in mid 2008, as fresh faced 21 year olds! When we met we were in the final year and, nights out with our own friends usually ended up at >**insert nightclub/bar**<. I'd been introduced to >**bride**< before but proceeded to bump into her and not have anything else to say (or shout) but, "Hi, alright??? How you doing??". What a natural, must get it from my father! I knew I wanted to speak to you and get to know you, but I had nothing else in my conversational locker than that. I thought then, and I still think, >**bride**< is 100% the most beautiful girl I have ever seen. She is the most beautiful person not just because she's stunning, but because she is the most caring, considerate, trustworthy and thoughtful person around, which I am sure you'll all agree. As I like to call her, she's a free range, good egg. She always puts others before herself and that's why she has so many close friends ... and that's why so many people want to be friends with her. After a few awkward conversations and impromtu passings by, **I asked** >**bride**< **out** (to see >**insert film title**< at the cinema). We soon knew our personalities were well and truly matched... and I could tell we were onto a winner. I took >**bride**< as my girlfriend to the May ball in 2009 at university (With >**university friends**<- great memories guys!). I was so proud of being with you and couldn't believe how lucky I was! Since then the rest is history, but history that I will briefly detail.*

- *For two years we lived 263 miles apart while boyfriend and girlfriend (so was the distance between >**city name**< and >**city name**<). After many train journeys from us both, >**bride**< made the decision to come down to >**city name**< to live with me and work while I pursued my rugby career. After a year we took the leap of faith and went... as I would call it.... **'up north'.** At least for a Cornish lad it was **'up north'**! We've been lucky to spend a lot of time seeing more of >**bride's**< Midlands-based family in the last 3 years, particularly **nanny! Hi Nan!***

- *We have also met (and got to know) some fantastic people over the last 3 years from our Midlands base. I've mentioned >**insert colleague's names**< for me..... now I can include for us both: >**insert friends' names**<.*

- *We have a brilliant life together in Solihull with Jelly the cat, and more recently joined by Max the dog and Ripley the horse. Our horse doesn't live with us... but >**bride**< wishes he did.*

- *Some of you may not know that >**bride**< and I have lived parallel lives. We were born on the same day so we share the same birthday (on >**insert date**< – born only 7 hours apart). >**Bride**< is older -I think I've caught up in height since! We had our appendix out at the same time before we knew each other aged 19. These are just two of the coincidences that are freakishly similar between us.*

- *>**Bride**<, I love you with all my heart and you are, as my nickname for you suggests, in every sense, 'gorgeous'. You are my soulmate and I can't begin to think of my life without you in it! Your generosity and your selflessness is on a level unlike any other person I have ever met. You're supportive, caring, loving, ...and I can't wait for us to continue our lives together as husband and wife.*

- *Now... A toast please ... to the gorgeous, >**bride's full married name**<!"*

Chapter Eleven

Introduction of best man

Congratulations - you have nearly completed your wedding speech! The last act for you to do is now introduce the best man as he prepares for his speech. You *could* simply introduce him by name; but remember - this is an opportunity to informally introduce him as a good mate, and warn the guests of what rubbish he is about to talk about you! Traditionally, the best man will start his speech with formalities then cut to the chase of embarrassing you as much as possible.

- *"Now, I'd like to take a moment to introduce your next speaker, my best man, >**insert best man's name**<. I've flattered him so far, and his ego may be slightly inflated. For those who are fans of the TV show Bad Education - he is the embodiment of Alfie Wickers (a slapstick character on British TV). .....For those familiar with children's TV he is your poor man's Mr Tumble (another slapstick character on British TV).*

I knew that he had done a degree in journalism, which led me to construct the last part of my speech...

- *He is currently, by profession, a maths teacher, but believe it or not his undergraduate degree is in broadcast journalism! So you now all know....... not to believe a word he says!!! Thank you and have a great day everyone!* ****hands microphone over to best man*.***

The last bullet point, where I reveal my best man was a journalist, was amazing ammunition for this joke. But here's the thing, you can use it also with the correct wording/delivery. You could always adapt this for anyone who hasn't done a journalism degree by saying (insinuating) that the best man once worked for a specific and notorious tabloid paper. Even though it's not true, it makes the joke work.

The upside to finishing on a joke is that you can say, "thank you everyone!" at the end of your speech, and as you are handing the microphone over people will take that as a cue to give applause while hopefully laughing already. It's a natural way of handing over on your terms, and be the perfect nudge for the guests to clap. You could put a completely different joke in to do with the fact that your best man has a habit of lying or stretching the truth, or at the least simply introduce him by name and then add, "*I hope he is kind to me now!*"

Chapter Twelve

Wedding day advice for the groom

You have now planned your speech (or are about to do so), and you are getting ready for the day. Whether it is two years away or two days away, I would like to pass on some personal advice for soon-to-be husbands for the day itself. My advice is limited to the wedding day only. The wedding night and beyond is up to you.

In the lead up to the day you will have you're your invitations, designed seating plans and deliberated over the guest list. You will have spoken to the catering company and will have the venue host's number on speed dial. You and your bride-to-be will have planned the best possible celebration of your marriage.

Your speech will only serve to solidify your reputation within both families. The fact you have prepared it so well will mean so much to a lot of people. The focus of a wedding is traditionally on the bride, the dress, and the food – yet nobody actually tells you, the groom, how to prepare yourself for the day. I will reveal what it was like from my point of view as the groom.

I recommend getting to know your photographer and meeting up in advance of the wedding day. I appreciate you may think this unnecessary, but it's completely worth it in terms of how your photos come out.

Most wedding photographers will offer a pre-wedding shoot package which not only allows you both to get used to the camera, but also get to know how your photographer operates to make images seem as natural as possible. Our photographer Rob gave us simple stances and poses to make sure that on the day we were able to go on auto-pilot when he was there. This sort of thing is not usually at the top of the groom's list of things to do ahead of the wedding, but meeting your photographer beforehand will make you relaxed and have the best possible photos to remember the day by.

My wife and I did do a pre-wedding shoot. We are both naturally introverted, and the pre-shoot made us feel much more comfortable on our wedding day. We also managed to get some great pictures of us (and our dog!) at a beautiful National Trust site that we could keep forever.

The day before your wedding you will hopefully have some quiet family time once the essentials are in place. The decorations will be put up, your suit laid out ready for the big day, and your nearest and dearest will be starting to arrive. A lot of people will ask you how you're feeling. They will ask questions like "*how you are coping?*". They ask with the best intentions (to appear supportive), but some ask with the assumption that it is only a matter of time before you have a nervous moment or a mini breakdown - which you might not have considered until they had asked! Take it in your stride and don't let other people make you feel stressed or pressured. Keep calm and be excited by the things you are most looking forward to.

It's important to get a good night's sleep the day before. Make it a priority, as you will be up and entertaining guests for over twelve hours the following day. I have heard horror stories of grooms that have gone for a 'quiet few' drinks the night before and have been horrendously tender the morning of their wedding. It's natural with friends you won't have seen for a while potentially on site or staying near you on the eve of the big day. Pre-decide on a bed time, stick to it, and don't have an excessive amount of alcohol. You will need a clear head and you won't want your memories of your wedding morning to be tainted by a huge hangover. Unless you are fine with that, in which case, go for it!

You will more than likely be staying separate from your fiancé the night before the wedding, so playing computer games or spending some down-time with friends is a good idea. This will keep your mind occupied without over-exerting yourself!

In the morning of your wedding, you will probably get ready with all of your groom's party. It may seem obvious, but make sure you eat all pre-ceremony food in your regular clothes to save spillages on your wedding suits! On the day it would be a disastrous mistake if you forget or try to rush a 'quick bite' when suited and booted.

The bridal party might take all morning to get ready - some brides get up at 6am or earlier for hair and make-up. You probably won't (get up this early), but make sure you allow enough time to do things you will only do on your wedding day. Set aside time for the fiddly bits and pieces such as putting on button-hole flowers, fitting your cuff links and tying your tie. I needed to go on YouTube to learn how to tie a Windsor knot, when I could have practiced and left this knot already perfectly made the night before. Doing these things last minute is not ideal and is not what you need to occupy your mind with.

The beginning of the day is essentially coordinated by the groom and the groom's party, as they are expected to greet the hired personnel such as the caterers and photographers, as well as the guests. The groomsmen are usually present on site ahead of the time of the ceremony. I advise you decide well before the day what roles your ushers and best man should take on the morning of your wedding, so you don't have to worry about last minute coordination. For example, ask your best man to speak to the venue host first thing, and ask an usher to take care of the photographer. Prepare your groomsmen for these roles, and they will know what is expected of them.

Your registrar or church service will usually conduct separate meetings with the bride and groom an hour or two before the wedding ceremony, to prove your identities and that you are legally able to wed. Don't be alarmed by any direct questioning, as they can be blunt and to the point. Once this formality is over, the ceremony will soon start.

With regard to the entrance of the bride, I know a lot of wedding guests take this as an opportunity to watch for the groom's reaction to seeing their fiancé in their dress for the first time. You will obviously be delighted to see your bride after a day or so apart, so remember to smile and get ready to enjoy the ceremony!

When your wedding ceremony ends, make sure you have already allocated someone to work with the photographer and have a list prepared of all the different group/family shots you want. If left to chance, it will be a long-winded process and can lead to frustration if it's cold outside! Try to make this as quick and efficient as possible. Assigning an efficient usher or the best man to work with the photographer is always a great idea (although efficient groomsmen are hard to find!).

Throughout the day, you will naturally want to talk at length with all of your guests. Depending on how big your guest list is, you may simply not have enough time, so don't worry if you don't get to catch up with everybody. You will be able to catch up in the weeks/months after with your closest friends, so try to prioritise seeing those you don't see very often, like family and friends who have travelled long distances. If you want to see as many people as possible, you can limit yourself to a few minutes per guest, having a 'closing line' such as, *"it's lovely to see you, thanks for coming"*. Guests know you will be in demand and won't be offended by your brevity.

Don't build up the importance of your speech in your own mind. You may find yourself dwelling on it or getting daunted, but remember, you have read this book and will prepare excellently. You are completely ready!

It is worth doing a reading of your speech to groomsmen a week or two before. It's even advisable to read it to your cat, dog or any inanimate object. By practicing verbally you can sound out any minor things that need to be changed or added, as well as time yourself. I know some grooms who wrote their speech the night before on a scrap of paper or even hurriedly on the day. Doing this can make your speech seem rushed, you might not be confident and it will be something you had wished you had put more time into.

There is usually some down-time between a traditional wedding breakfast and the evening guests arriving. During this time I suggest you and your new wife take a minute to have a cup of tea or relax! You will have had a very busy day and you will appreciate some time together to take it all in and settle down. I would suggest planning this in otherwise you won't do it. Trust me, just taking twenty minutes to relax in a quiet lounge will refresh you both, get you off your feet and enable you to have energy for the rest of the evening's antics.

Cutting the cake is an awkward formality and a rite of passage that most married couples are subjected to. It feels very awkward and it is just one of the photo opportunities that guests love, so just smile and wave!

Also, make a point of having some evening food; you will be surprised at how easily your time can be taken up by others who want to wish you well! You will have carefully selected the dining options for your guests; so why shouldn't you take some time to enjoy it for yourselves?

The first dance is something you may wish to practice together. However, my advice is that it is completely unnecessary unless you particularly want to show something off, or if you are, unlike me, very good at dancing! It is perfectly acceptable to sway slowly around the dancefloor, there is no need to do anything elaborate. Within a minute or two you will have everyone else around you anyway.

The evening will go very quickly, so it will be up to you to get the right balance between mingling with your close friends and those who you don't often see. You will feel like you are on official duties, but remember to enjoy yourself! The day is should be enjoyed for every minute, and is the first day of your new lives together. Make sure you soak it all up, and take some moments to step back and reflect on the occasion you and your partner have created. I'm sure that you'll have the best day of your life.

Chapter Thirteen

Extra Jokes you could use

Although I didn't use these jokes in my speech, these are some of the best ones I left on the cutting room floor. I've heard these (or similar) across all the weddings I have ever been to. You may find they come in handy, so take your pick if you wish!

- *"For a good speech I'm told the speaker needs to stand up to be seen, speak up to be heard, then sit down and shut up!"*

- Props can be used if there's a time and a place for them. I know a groom who got out their new wife's oldest and most favourite teddy bear, and follow it with saying something like, *"I hope I can live up to your clearly high standards as a life partner!"*

- *(On the best man/ushers)* – *"My ushers and best man all did a runner last night – so I'd like to introduce their stand-ins!"*

- *(On the best man/ushers)* – *"They are all dressed so smartly because they've just come here straight from court this morning. Crimes against hairstyles".*

- *Now, William Shakespeare was once quoted as saying, "If music be the food of love, then play on". Lovely, but have you seen Dad's dancing?! There's an exception to every rule.*

- One that's always gone down well is the use of the bride or best man's old school report (or a scrap of paper that pretends to be!). You could relate your bride's current interests to their old subjects at school to get a laugh. Get their family to dig it up. It's a universally understood medium for people to get on board with understanding.

- *(To new in-laws)* *"A lot of men have said they've had a bad experience with getting to know their new in-laws, but I have gained the perfect second set of parents. I couldn't be happier. (*looks to in-laws) Maggie and Bob, did I read that OK?"*

Thank you for reading this book!

It would mean the world to me if you could take the time to rate this book (out of five stars) and post a quick review on Amazon.

All reviews (good or bad) help me reach more people online.

Thank you!

Steve

P.S. I'd love to hear how your speech goes on your big day. Please drop me a line by emailing stevedeanjohns@outlook.com or finding me on twitter: @SteveJohnsey.

Chapter Fourteen

Steve's speech in full

- *"Good afternoon everyone! We take great pleasure in welcoming you here for our special day... where the countdown is over... and we are now Mr & Mrs >**surname**<! (pause for applause!)"*

- *"On behalf of my wife and I (!!!) we want to thank you all for being here with us on this special day, for all your good wishes, and for your wonderful gifts. People have travelled from various parts of the UK to be with us today... we have large groups of people from Cornwall and Devon, Essex and London, and the Midlands, among others".*

- *"For a while we've looked forward to bringing all the people that are special to us together, and now you're here, all scrubbed up and smelling nice. It's surreal for me to speak to you all at the same time. The fact that you are all here means everything to us.*

- *Just a bit of housekeeping – please make sure your glasses are charged for any toasts. Please stay in your seats for toasts from me – just raising a glass is fine! I have a few gifts to hand out later so when I do, a big clap would be great please!"*
  - *"We holidayed as 'family >**family surname (e.g. Smith)**<' in Florida in the summer of 2012 .... it was incredible! One incident made me think I was truly part of the family.... (mention the theme park and breaking the*

wine bottles in the evening – hope they have forgiven me!).

- *>**mother of bride**< - You, >**mother of the bride's partner**< and >**bride's sister**< have all made me feel so welcome since the beginning and I am so lucky to have married your daughter today, who is the most beautiful person to me in every sense. I'd also like to say how wonderful both you and my own mum look today, and I'm sure everyone else agrees! (*cue cheers/whoops).*

- *I would now like us now to raise a toast to >**bride's**< father, >**bride's father (who is no longer with us)**<. Although I never had the pleasure of meeting him, I am told we are alike in many ways and I hope he would have approved of >**bride's**< choice of husband. I know he would be very, very proud of you. A toast please… to >**bride's father (who is no longer with us)**<. Thank you all.*

- *To Mum, Dad, >**mother of bride**< and >**mother of the bride's partner**<, Thank you for everything you've done towards making today a success. We really appreciate you being there for us and we wanted to give you a little something to thank you. *Hand presents*. A round of applause please for our family.*

- *"Personally now, I'd like to say a thank you to my wonderful parents or, as I like to say in my* *strongest Cornish accent, **motheeeeer** and **faaather**! I owe so much to you both, all the evenings and the long trips to hundreds of rugby pitches across the country in my youth, and generally for kicking me out of bed in time for school.*

- *Dad- you have been an inspiration to me with your work ethic and drive to develop the business and you have put in some crazy hours, I still don't know how you got by with as little sleep! When I was a toddler Dad used to make me hot chocolate at 5.30am each morning before going to work. I am thankful for you and mum giving me the opportunity to pursue my passions of rugby and sport, which has led to a career in these fields.*

- *Mum, as I've said, you look amazing today. My main aim with this bit is to make you cry! You have always been the caring, rational, supportive and loving person watching over me and helping me with anything, from washing rugby kit, to your help with certain school projects. You too are an inspiration in so many ways. Thank you for everything.*

- *"Now with ladies first, I would like to continue in traditional fashion by thanking our maid of honour, >**bride's**< sister, >**bride's sister's name**< and all of our bridesmaids. I know you'll **(addressing audience)** all agree that they all look beautiful!" (cue some whooping and clapping by lifting the tone of your voice at the end of the sentence).*

- *">**Bride's sister**< (also **Maid of honour**), you have always been with >**bride**< in both the good times **and** the tough times as her sister, and always been there for **us** both with advice, support and a lot of laughs. Thanks for everything you have done for us (including for our wedding), you have put in a great deal of work that we both appreciate. Also, to the bridesmaids >**Bridesmaid 1**< (my sister), >**Bridesmaid 2**< and >**Bridesmaid 3**<, thanks for all of your support for >**bride**<, she loves each of you dearly, and we value each of you immensely.*

  - *>**Bridesmaid 1**<, 'sis', even though I still think you are 12 (and I still treat you like you're 12!!!), you have grown up into a beautiful young lady. Now you, >**bride**< and >**bride's sister**< are officially sisters! Ahh!*

  - *We hope you enjoyed opening your gifts this morning with >**bride**<. A toast please… to… the bridesmaids!"*

  - *"Onto my groom's party today. They are all here for their companionship; clearly not for their brains or beauty!"*

  - *">**Best man**<, thanks for everything you have done in preparation for today, including an incredible stag do in >**place name**<. >**Best man**<, we go back to our primary school days playing football against each other for >**school*** *name<! We were part of the infamous backstreet boys tribute dance group in a school concert (**addressing audience**) - I am still as shocked as you lot are! We have been solid mates for a long long time. We may not have seen each other as much as we'd have liked to because of where we've lived recently.... but whenever we meet up it is as if no time has passed. (Addressing audience) Believe it or not, >**Best man**< has worked as a manager for L'Oréal shampoo. I'd like to say thanks for being my best man by giving you a little something too. Because you're worth it. Cheers mate". ***Hand present***.*

- *"Thanks also to my ushers- my brother >**Usher 1**<, then there's >**Usher 2**< and >**Usher 3**<. You guys have been fantastic not only today but throughout my life as mates".*

- *>**Usher 1, also my brother**<, it means so much that you could be my usher today. I want to thank you for always being there to support me and scrap with me (and beat me up many times).You watched over me like a hawk as I cut the lawn (as a quality assurance measure of course), and generally looked after all things in the business when dad went 'gallivanting' on his rugby away days (***turn to dad*** you still do that don't you?). A 3 hour trip to where we live is apparently 'do-able in a day!'. >**Usher 1**<, we had some great times growing up spending days out with cousins (all of which are here today!) with Granny, Grampy, Granddad and our <u>amazing</u> Grandma and Auntie Sylvia. Hi Grandma and Auntie*

Sylvia! **>Usher 1<**, *you have been caring and kind - >**bride**< loves the fact she now has a brother!* ***Hand present*.**

- **>Usher 2<**, *when you arrived at >**secondary school name**< in Year 9... with long blonde golden locks (***audience should now laugh as he is now bald***).... you were the quickest kid on a rugby pitch I had ever seen, and had a thick northern accent. Where's that gone!? We had some great times throughout school, at Uni and ever since then. You can all ask >**Usher 2**< later to see pictures of his infamous 'dreadlock' phase. It will be well worth it I promise you! Please accept my gift as a thanks.* ***Hand present*.**

- **>Usher 3<**, *you've been there since I started working at >**insert workplace**< – you and >**insert girlfriend's name**< have been great friends to >**bride**< and I. You have always been there at the drop of a hat, and along with >**other colleague**< and >**other colleague**< you have made sure I have stayed sane at work – and made sure that I have a laugh too! Not only have* __we__ *enjoyed your company, but we have a golden Labrador who also loves you very much! (good job too, because you're the one that convinced us to get him!). Please may I give you a little something for being my usher today.* ***Hand Present***

- *A toast please to ... the groom's party".*

- *"May I also say a big thanks to our beautiful flower girls for helping us today! >**flower girl 1**<, >**flower girl 2**< and >**flower girl 3**<.... you all look amazing. A round of applause please for the flower girls! We are so happy that we have altogether so many children at our wedding; you really make it special as we've got to know each of you and seen you grow up!".*

- *"We wanted to thank the >**venue name**< for hosting our wedding today. We've been in awe of the place since we first saw it! Also thanks to >**catering company name**<, our amazing caterers today. That roast beef was amazing! By the way, we went to a 'taster' day to 'sample' our food - I had one of those joints to myself and I couldn't breathe after!!! In appreciation for both our venue and caterers please could we give a round of applause".*

- *"Most importantly today, I wanted to thank >**Bride's new, full married name**< for agreeing to marry me! As >**mother of the bride**< has already said, she is beautiful, she's kind, she's caring and loving... and I still can't believe how lucky I am to now be able to call her my wife!*

- ***addressing bride*** >**bride**<, I want to take this moment to share some of our story so far with everyone. (addressing audience) Don't panic!*

- *We met through mutual friends at University in mid 2008, as fresh faced 21 year olds! When we met we were in the final year and, nights out with our own friends usually ended up at >**insert nightclub/bar**<. I'd been introduced to >**bride**< before but proceeded to bump into her and not have anything else to say (or shout) but, "Hi, alright??? How you doing??". What a natural, must get it from my father! I knew I wanted to speak to you and get to know you, but I had nothing else in my conversational locker than that. I thought then, and I still think, >**bride**< is 100% the most beautiful girl I have ever seen. She is the most beautiful person not just because she's stunning, but because she is the most caring, considerate, trustworthy and thoughtful person around, which I am sure you'll all agree. As I like to call her, she's a free range, good egg. She always puts others before herself and that's why she has so many close friends ... and that's why so many people want to be friends with her. After a few awkward conversations and impromtu passings by, **I asked** >**bride**< **out** (to see >**insert film title**< at the cinema). We soon knew our personalities were well and truly matched... and I could tell we were onto a winner. I took >**bride**< as my girlfriend to the May ball in 2009 at university (With >**university friends**<- great memories guys!). I was so proud of being with you and couldn't believe how lucky I was! Since then the rest is history, but history that I will briefly detail.*

- *For two years we lived 263 miles apart while boyfriend and girlfriend (so was the distance between >city name< and >city name<). After many train journeys from us both, >bride< made the decision to come down to >city name< to live with me and work while I pursued my rugby career. After a year we took the leap of faith and went... as I would call it.... 'up north'. At least for a Cornish lad it was 'up north'! We've been lucky to spend a lot of time seeing more of >bride's< Midlands-based family in the last 3 years, particularly nanny! Hi Nan!*

- *We have also met (and got to know) some fantastic people over the last 3 years from our Midlands base. I've mentioned >insert colleague's names< for me..... now I can include for us both: >insert friends' names<.*

- *We have a brilliant life together in Solihull with Jelly the cat, and more recently joined by Max the dog and Ripley the horse. Our horse doesn't live with us... but >bride< wishes he did.*

- *Some of you may not know that >bride< and I have lived parallel lives. We were born on the same day so we share the same birthday (on >insert date< – born only 7 hours apart). >Bride< is older -I think I've caught up in height since! We had our appendix out at the same time before we knew each other aged 19. These are just two of the coincidences that are freakishly similar between us.*

- *>**Bride**<, I love you with all my heart and you are, as my nickname for you suggests, in every sense, 'gorgeous'. You are my soulmate and I can't begin to think of my life without you in it! Your generosity and your selflessness is on a level unlike any other person I have ever met. You're supportive, caring, loving, ...and I can't wait for us to continue our lives together as husband and wife.*

- *Now... A toast please ... to the gorgeous, >**bride's full married name**<!*

- *"Now, I'd like to take a moment to introduce your next speaker, my best man, >**insert best man's name**<. I've flattered him so far, and his ego may be slightly inflated. For those who are fans of the TV show Bad Education - he is the embodiment of Alfie Wickers (a slapstick character on British TV). .....For those familiar with children's TV he is your poor man's Mr Tumble (another slapstick character on British TV).*

- *He is currently, by profession, a maths teacher, but believe it or not his undergraduate degree is in broadcast journalism! So you now all know....... not to believe a word he says!!! Thank you and have a great day everyone! *hands microphone over to best man*.*

Thank you for reading this book!

It would mean the world to me if you could take the time to rate this book (out of five stars) and post a quick review on Amazon.

All reviews (good or bad) help me reach more people online.

Thank you!

Steve

P.S. I'd love to hear how your speech goes on your big day. Please drop me a line by emailing stevedeanjohns@outlook.com or finding me on twitter: @SteveJohnsey.